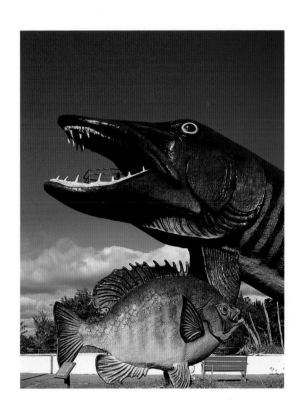

CAROL M. HIGHSMITH AND TED LANDPHAIR

WISCONSIN

A PHOTOGRAPHIC TOUR

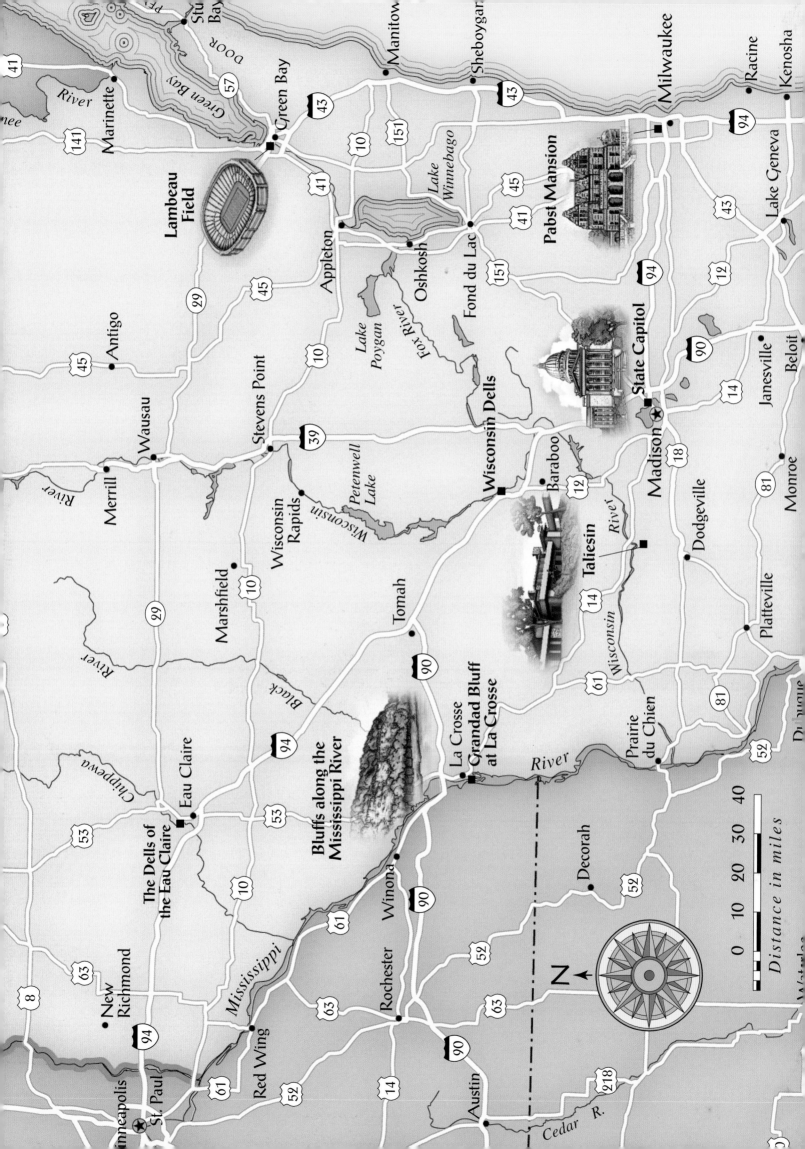

CRESCENT BOOKS

NEW YORK

FRONT COVER: Because most Wisconsin farmers keep dairy herds on their trim farmsteads, silos punctuate the landscape. Another ten could be seen out of camera range beyond this farm near Leland, south of Baraboo. BACK COVER: Dells Mill, built in 1864 near Augusta, operated as a flour and feed mill for more than one hundred years. It has been in the Clark family for four generations and is now a museum. PAGE 1: The elusive muskie is a tenacious fighter and a prize catch. This 143-foot-long, walk-through fiberglass and steel specimen towers over the National Fresh Water Fishing Hall of Fame in Hayward, where hundreds of U.S.- and world-record catches are mounted. PAGES 2–3: The Mississippi River cuts a wide swath near Maiden Rock in beautiful bluffs country.

This 1998 edition is published by Crescent Books®, an imprint of Random House Value Publishing, Inc., 201 East 50th Street, New York, N. Y 10022.

Crescent Books® and design are registered trademarks of Random House Value Publishing, Inc.

Random House
New York • Toronto • London • Sydney • Auckland
http://www.randomhouse.com/

Printed and bound in China

Library of Congress Cataloging-in-Publication Data
Highsmith, Carol M., 1946–
Wisconsin / Carol M. Highsmith and Ted Landphair.
p.   cm. — (A photographic tour)
Includes index.
ISBN 0-517-20181-X (hc: alk. paper)
1. Wisconsin—Tours. 2. Wisconsin—Pictorial works. 3. Wisconsin—Description and travel. I. Landphair, Ted, 1942–   . II. Title. III. Series: Highsmith, Carol M., 1946–   Photographic tour.
F579.3.H54   1998   97–40013
917.7504´43—dc21   CIP

8 7 6 5 4 3

Project Editor: Donna Lee Lurker
Designed by Robert L. Wiser, Archetype Press, Inc., Washington, D.C.

THE AUTHORS GRATEFULLY ACKNOWLEDGE THE SUPPORT PROVIDED BY

HILTON HOTELS CORPORATION

AND

THE MILWAUKEE RIVER HILTON INN
THE OSHKOSH HILTON

IN CONNECTION WITH THE COMPLETION OF THIS BOOK

THE AUTHORS ALSO WISH TO THANK THE FOLLOWING FOR THEIR GENEROUS ASSISTANCE AND HOSPITALITY DURING THEIR VISITS TO WISCONSIN

Wisconsin Department of Tourism

Greater Madison Convention & Visitors Bureau

Greater Milwaukee Convention and Visitors Bureau

Wisconsin Dells Visitor and Convention Bureau

Best Western, Wausau

Brookstone Inn, La Crosse

Country Inn & Suites, Hayward

Round Barn Lodge and Restaurant, Spring Green

Linda Bjorklund and Tom Blanck, Stockholm

John Gurda, Milwaukee

John Patrick Hunter, Madison

Bob Lee, Menomonie

Carlton McKinney, Edina, Minnesota

Dr. Fred Olson, Wauwatosa

Kathleen Ratican, Minnetonka, Minnesota

Dr. William F. Thompson, Madison

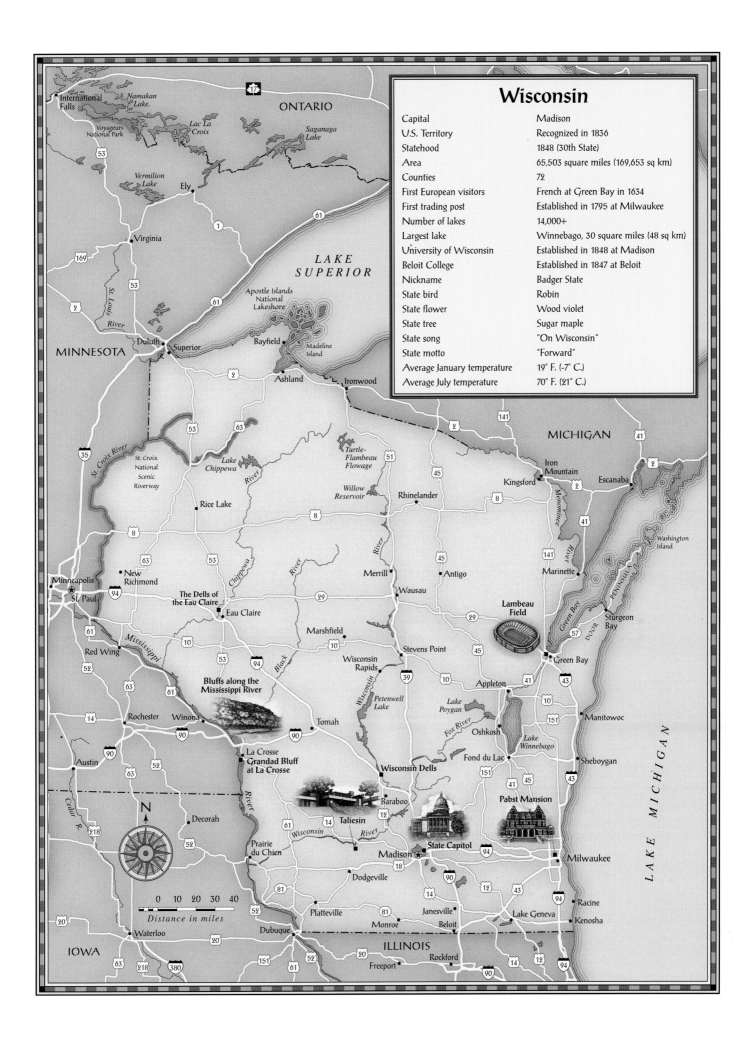

Wisconsin

Capital	Madison
U.S. Territory	Recognized in 1836
Statehood	1848 (30th State)
Area	65,503 square miles (169,653 sq km)
Counties	72
First European visitors	French at Green Bay in 1634
First trading post	Established in 1795 at Milwaukee
Number of lakes	14,000+
Largest lake	Winnebago, 30 square miles (48 sq km)
University of Wisconsin	Established in 1848 at Madison
Beloit College	Established in 1847 at Beloit
Nickname	Badger State
State bird	Robin
State flower	Wood violet
State tree	Sugar maple
State song	"On Wisconsin"
State motto	"Forward"
Average January temperature	19° F. (-7° C.)
Average July temperature	70° F. (21° C.)

ONTARIO

MINNESOTA

LAKE SUPERIOR

MICHIGAN

LAKE MICHIGAN

IOWA

ILLINOIS

International Falls
Namakan Lake
Lac La Croix
Saganaga Lake
Voyageurs National Park
Vermilion Lake
Ely
Virginia
Apostle Islands National Lakeshore
Madeline Island
Bayfield
Duluth
Superior
St. Louis River
Ashland
Ironwood
Iron Mountain
Kingsford
Escanaba
Washington Island
Turtle-Flambeau Flowage
Lake Chippewa
Willow Reservoir
Rhinelander
Antigo
St. Croix National Scenic Riverway
St. Croix River
Rice Lake
Chippewa River
Merrill
Wausau
Marinette
Menominee River
DOOR PENINSULA
New Richmond
Minneapolis
St. Paul
The Dells of the Eau Claire
Eau Claire
Marshfield
Stevens Point
Wisconsin Rapids
Lambeau Field
Green Bay
Sturgeon Bay
Red Wing
Mississippi
Black River
Petenwell Lake
Appleton
Manitowoc
Bluffs along the Mississippi River
Rochester
Winona
Tomah
Lake Poygan
Oshkosh
Lake Winnebago
Sheboygan
Fox River
Fond du Lac
Austin
La Crosse
Grandad Bluff at La Crosse
Wisconsin Dells
Decorah
Baraboo
Taliesin
Pabst Mansion
Cedar R.
Prairie du Chien
Wisconsin River
State Capitol
Madison
Milwaukee
Dodgeville
Lake Geneva
Racine
Kenosha
Waterloo
Platteville
Monroe
Janesville
Beloit
Dubuque
Rockford
Freeport

N

0 10 20 30 40
Distance in miles

WISCONSIN, WITH ITS EMERALD HILLSIDES, rushing rivers, rugged bluffs, deep woods, and well mannered, educated, and industrious people, has been called "the perfect state." And the tens of thousands of visitors who each year raft Wisconsin's rapids or tour its Dells, hunt Wisconsin deer or bear, camp in its rugged parks, make tracks in a snowmobile, and sail Wisconsin's rippling lakes or poke holes in a frozen one—perchance to snare a passing pike—cheerfully agree.

Wisconsin borders two Great Lakes, holds eighty-five hundred smaller ones, dots its horizons with innumerable silos and a few respectable skyscrapers, and boasts four delightfully distinguishable seasons, ideal for agriculture. One hundred fifty growing days are average in all but the extreme Northern Highland. Winters are long, Wisconsinites admit with a wink, especially in the Northwoods. That's what mittens and snowshoes, cross-country skis and snow tires were made for. Great forests of birch and pine, ash and maple have at last been preserved, a century after logging cartels and greedy railroads, abetted by corrupt politicians, stripped the northern landscape of trees. It was this "robber baron" legacy that spawned Wisconsin's fabled Progressive Movement, led by Madison lawyer Robert A. La Follette Sr. and preserved by his sons: "Young Bob," who held his father's old Senate seat for twenty-one years after Old Bob's death in 1925; and Phil, who won the Wisconsin governorship three times. Today, responsible harvesting supports bustling plywood, pulp, and paper plants across the state's northern reaches, and respect for the environment is a Wisconsin trademark. John Muir, founder of the Sierra Club and a crusader for America's national park system, was the prototype Wisconsin environmentalist. He wrote in luxuriant detail of the birds whose songs "sweeten Wisconsin."

The state has established a wildlife refuge in the desolate Horicon Marsh—the "Everglades of the North"—whose thirty-two-thousand acres of cattails and duckweed are a popular stop for a quarter of a million migrating Canada geese. Controls on industrial emissions are vigilantly maintained, and visitors to Wisconsin are hard-pressed to find an unkempt wayside—as rest stops are called in these parts—or discarded cheeseburger wrappers along a highway. Wisconsin's state parks are spacious and more than a touch wild, full of hiking trails, waterfalls, and glorious vistas of valleys, rocky deposits called kettle moraines, and teardrop-shaped hills known as "drumlins," all formed by glaciers ages ago.

Wisconsin has produced remarkable sons and daughters, and a number of firsts. Escape artist Harry Houdini, painter Georgia O'Keeffe, hero pilot Billy Mitchell, novelist Edna Ferber, outboard engine inventor Ole Evinrude, actors Frederic March and Spencer Tracy, actor and director Orson Welles, sportswriter Red Smith, and innovative architect Frank Lloyd Wright were all born or spent significant years in Wisconsin. America's first kindergarten and vocational schools, its first traveling library and direct primary, and the first railroad rights-of-way turned into hiking and biking trails turned up in the Badger State. Christopher Latham Sholes, a Wisconsinite, put together the first typewriter in Milwaukee in 1867. Wisconsin was the first state to number its highways, the first to require seat belts in new cars, and the first to outlaw the death penalty and to revoke the Ku Klux Klan's charter. First, too, with worker's compensation and unemployment laws, yet first as well, in the 1990s, to have a go at "ending welfare as we know it" with tough "Wisconsin works" legislation. This effort, spurred by Governor Tommy Thompson, was made all the more remarkable by the state's reputation—shared by its Minnesota neighbor and by California—as a welfare haven, where generous benefits were said to

Two University of Wisconsin–Stout art professors, who called themselves "The Arts People," painted this mural on a wall of Lee's Drug Store in Menomonie. Borrowing the setting from an old photograph that pictured lumber barons and other wealthy burghers, the artists substituted farmers, bricklayers, homemakers, and others whom they felt really built Wisconsin.

Milwaukeeans built stately homes along Lake Michigan, and they have long promenaded along its shores. This is Juneau Park about 1910. The Chicago & North Western Railroad depot is in the distance.

draw newcomers like a porch light draws moths. One reason attempts to put welfare recipients to work resonated in Wisconsin was the remarkable economic turnaround of Indian reservations, where even non-Indian unemployment fell sharply as Indian casinos brought dollars and jobs to the poorest parts of the state.

Wisconsin is the only state in which a major-league sports franchise—football's Green Bay Packers—is owned not by a well-heeled mogul or corporate conglomerate, but by a couple thousand local stockholders, none of whom ever sees any profits. They're immediately plowed back into the team, and thus into the community. Because of that sense of shared ownership, as much as the Packers' status as an original NFL franchise with multiple Super Bowl wins (wrapped around maddeningly fallow seasons), fans in "Titletown, U.S.A." and throughout Wisconsin define *fan*atical. From the coulees of southwest Wisconsin to the pines up north, car banners and convenience-store windows, diehards' game-day faces, and even pumpkins are jovially painted Packer green and gold, even before the first acorn falls. It has not hurt "the Pack," either, that it gets to play teams from warm-weather cities on the "frozen tundra" it knows so well, or that the basketball Bucks and baseball Brewers are based in Milwaukee—a suspicious place in the minds of rural sports fans—and that Wisconsin has no big-league hockey team at all.

"Good Wisconsin stock," as the people sometimes refer to themselves, revere the hearth-and-home values of the Jeffersonian yeoman farmer. After all, it was in a "Little House in the Big Woods"—Wisconsin woods—that "Pa" first taught Laura Ingalls Wilder, and she, in turn, taught generations of the nation's children, the virtues of hard work and fair dealing through her novels. The state symbol, the tenacious badger, embodies Wisconsinites' determination to build and live a good life.

Remarkably, Wisconsin is one of America's most Catholic states yet also one of the most Lutheran states. Its roots are notably German and Scandinavian, but many cultures have blossomed here. Milwaukee alone holds Polish, Irish, Italian, and German fests; "Asian Moon" and "African World" festivals, a Mexican fiesta, "Serbian Days," and a Native American celebration called "Indian Summer" each year. Racine, with the nation's highest concentration of Danish descendants, throws an annual "Kringle Fest," named for its sinfully delicious filled Danish pastry. Not too far from Madison are "Little Norway" in Blue Mounds and "America's Little Switzerland" in New Glarus. There's a "Little Finland" cultural center in Hayward, and colorful powwows on the Menominee and Chippewa reservations in the western and northern parts of the state. Little wonder Wisconsin's Heritage Tourism program, begun in 1990, has become a model for similar efforts nationwide.

Winter sports also draw enthusiasts of every nationality: cross-country skiing on frozen rivers, canals, and more than three hundred designated trails; ice-fishing jamborees on frozen lakes; a snowmobile derby at Eagle River; speedracing on skates at Beloit; and ski jumping at Westby near La Crosse. Wisconsin marks twenty thousand miles of interconnected snowmobile trails—ranked the best in North America. Wisconsinites and their guests also keep moving in wintertime with activities that only a few have seen and fewer have tried: windskiing across a frozen lake or field at speeds nearly three times the wind itself; windsailing; ice boating; and even "skijoring," which involves climbing onto a pair of skis and hitching to a sled dog team. Northern Wisconsin hosts the American Birkebeiner, the nation's largest cross-country ski marathon, each February.

It's not entirely true that Wisconsin cuisine is a cholesterol-fighter's nightmare. There's more to most diets than cheese and a "brat and a beer." Cheese, however, is certainly serious business in a state with more than three million dairy cows. For many years Wisconsin law forbade the sale of oleomargarine within its borders. Its dairy farmers produce more than two hundred varieties of cheese, two of them—colby and baby Swiss—Wisconsin creations, and a number, like Havarti, once thought to be exclusively foreign and exotic. And veal bratwursts, pork bratwursts, summer sausage that the locals call "beef logs," a half-dozen kinds of wieners, and a dozen more obscure varieties of wursts still hang from hooks in old-fashioned meat markets across the state.

Wisconsin farmers had little choice but to turn to dairying. Wheat was the Badger State's early cash crop, and Wisconsin was the Union Army's breadbasket in the Civil War, to which the state also contributed almost one hundred thousand soldiers. But no giant modern wheat combine could negotiate the hills and woods, and yields could not match those of Minnesota and the Dakotas. So most Wisconsin farmers turned their spreads over to cows and corn. In comparison with states to the south and west, most farms are still small, about two hundred acres on average, and stubbornly owner-occupied. But one sentimental symbol of the farmstead—the old dairy barn—is fast disappearing. Barns were designed to store hay bales on a second floor, from which the fodder would be tossed to cattle below. But as farm machinery enabled farmers to bundle hay in huge rolls, simple sheds—many prefabricated—have replaced drafty old barns on many farms.

Though state license plates proclaim Wisconsin's continuing status as "America's Dairyland," its economy for a century has revolved

Streetcars were a favored mode of transportation in Milwaukee. These rattled up and down Wisconsin Avenue at the turn of the twentieth century.

far more around heavy industry than on farming. Beer is not the bulwark, despite the stereotype, though for years Schlitz, Miller, and Pabst, in varying order, followed only Anheuser-Busch among America's producers of suds. Schlitz was absorbed by Stroh's, a Michigan brewer, after years of decline following an ill-advised change in its brew formula; and after 152 years Pabst—already a Stroh's label as well—closed its brewery in Milwaukee in 1996 and moved operations to La Crosse. But Miller solidified its hold on second place in national sales by beating Anheuser-Busch to the "lite" beer punch and by diversifying its brand line.

Bigger than beer are bathtubs in Kohler, floor wax in Racine, facial tissues in Appleton, motorcycles in Milwaukee, and cheese in Monroe. Meanwhile, makers of tractors and truck bodies, electric generators and diesel engines in Milwaukee, Kenosha, and Racine—out of the limelight because their products were not mass-marketed and were rarely advertised in the popular media—were outpacing all the Milwaukee brewers combined. That's not to say mergers, foreign competition, and recessions have not taken their toll. Wisconsin, which had topped two million in population for the first time in 1950, lost two hundred thousand people with the decline of Rust Belt industries over the forty years that followed. Now, more and more of Wisconsin's economy is service-based; graphics, insurance, computer, and financial-planning firms are prospering, and the state's public university system is one of the nation's largest. In recent years, agriculture—including fishing and forestry as well as farming—has accounted for less than *five percent* of the gross state product, industry around thirty percent, and services for all the rest.

Wisconsin is fastidious, with dozens of tidy, well gardened, chipper small cities. They're not chic like New York or trendy like Los Angeles—aren't trying to be—and Wisconsinites are quick to point out that their cities *certainly* haven't the corruption and congestion of that megalith to the south: Chicago. In their flat, faintly nasal accents, punctuating certain syllables ("Wis-SCON-sin," "Chi-CAWG-uh"), Wisconsin's citizens love to tweak Chicago, and to beat its teams in sports. Wisconsinites will tell you it's those Chicagoans (not Illinoisans in general) buying second homes who are driving up Wisconsin land prices, Chicagoans clogging Wisconsin's free highways with their cars and campers each weekend, but when we want to catch a concert down in Chicago, they make us pay tolls. Surely it was Chicagoans at the "U"—the University of Wisconsin in Madison—not our clean-cut kids from Oshkosh or Eau Claire, they'll say with a twinkle, who caused all the trouble back in the Sixties. And so forth. Of course the Wisconsin Department of Tourism knows what state is Chicago's playland, and it operates an office in the Windy City to help keep the drivers and their dollars coming. With the sharp decline in mining and forestry, tourism officials know full well that recreational visitors have become the salvation of northern Wisconsin's economy.

The first European known to set foot in what is now Wisconsin came not from the south but from the north. French explorer Jean Nicolet paddled into Green Bay from Quebec in 1634 looking for a Northwest Passage trade route to China. He went home disappointed, and it was a while before French trappers and traders followed. They coveted otter and beaver pelts, not land, and so while French place names abound in Wisconsin (La Crosse, Lac La Belle, Prairie du Chien, Trempealeau, Nicolet National Forest), it is a rare place that can trace

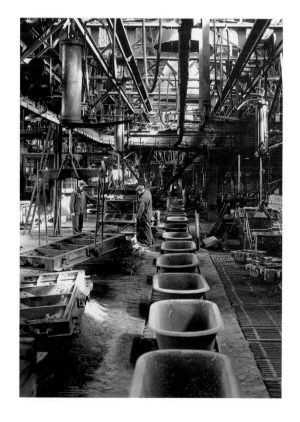

The Kohler Company, in the town of the same name near Sheboygan, supplies much of the world with bathroom fixtures, including these bathtubs rolling off the foundry production line in 1933.

its land ownership back to the French. The same lack of interest in real estate did not apply to the British who were victorious in the French and Indian Wars of the middle 1700s and nominally controlled this western edge of European settlement for a time. To them, and to American settlers who moved into southwest Wisconsin in search of lead after the British were expelled during the War of 1812, land—gained with or without native inhabitants' blessing—meant power. It was these miners whose practice of burrowing into hillside caves to spend the winter first earned Wisconsinites their "badger" nickname.

Indian treaties ceded most of present-day Wisconsin to whites by 1833, the year the first newspaper in Wisconsin (then still in Michigan Territory), the *Green Bay Intelligencer*, was established. Native Americans' final, futile stand had been the Black Hawk War, spilling northward into Wisconsin from the Rock River Valley of Illinois the year before. Among the U.S. soldiers dispatched to oust the Fox and Sauk tribes were Captain Abraham Lincoln, Lieutenant Jefferson Davis, and Henry Dodge—who would later be a territorial governor of Wisconsin. After bloody fighting, Chief Black Hawk and the remnants of his band were disarmed and forced west into Iowa. The proud Sauk leader spent his last years as a touring curiosity and a darling of Washington salon painters.

Wisconsin was, in rather quick order, part of the vast Northwest Territory, then of Indiana, Illinois, and Michigan territories in succession before becoming a U.S. territory of its own in 1836. For a time, Wisconsin encompassed parts of present-day Minnesota, North and South Dakota, and Iowa. With the coming of statehood as the Union's thirtieth state in 1848, Wisconsin settled into its present boundaries, stretching 280 miles west from Lake Michigan and 320 miles north from Illinois to Lake Superior. The new state took its name quite naturally from the

Works Progress Administration photographer Harold Hone snapped this view of the Wisconsin state capitol down State Street in 1939. The street is even busier today, and the 1927 Orpheum Theater is still in business.

Immigrants arrive in the Chippewa Valley by steamboat in 1868. Then just twenty years a state, Wisconsin afforded newcomers a great opportunity to build a life in new, bustling cities and on the farm.

Indian "Miskonsing" and French "Ouisconsin," meaning "gathering of the waters" and referring more to the wild Fox, Wisconsin, Rock, Saint Croix, and Mississippi rivers than to Wisconsin's many lakes.

After its initial Yankee settlement, Wisconsin became heavily German for a time, purely as a matter of timing. Just as feisty German "Forty-eighters" were fleeing the strife of Central Europe en masse in the mid-1800s, the United States was offering homesteaders one hundred sixty free acres to settle the mostly untamed state it had just created to the north of Illinois. Not only did these Germans find Wisconsin's climate and topography to their liking, save for a paucity of alps, the hardy Germans also quickly put Wisconsin's abundant raw materials to good use in machine shops, paper mills, and factories along Lake Michigan and in nearby river valleys. Norwegians and Swedes answered the same free-land invitation, but just a bit later. Thus they concentrated in the western part of the state and into Minnesota and the Dakotas. At the turn of the twentieth century, four of every five Wisconsinites had been born abroad; today, no more than five percent are foreign-born.

Wisconsin prospered agriculturally and industrially through the nineteenth century. A maverick reform movement led by Milwaukee socialists—"sewer socialists," as Milwaukeeans called them as a compliment for their campaigns for better city services—and the successful campaign for governor by Old Bob La Follette in 1901 brought waves of change, at first within the Republican Party under the "Progressive" banner. (His opponents within the party called themselves "Stalwarts.") The reform movement intensified when son Phil La Follette pulled the Progressives out of the Republican Party in 1934.

Wisconsin Republicans knew a lot about reform. The national party had been founded under that banner in tiny Ripon, Wisconsin, in 1854 after a local lawyer and abolitionist, Alvan E. Bovay, returned from a chat with his friend, New York editor Horace Greeley, at the Whig national convention. Bovay called a meeting of citizens in the little Ripon schoolhouse in order to remonstrate against the Kansas-Nebraska Act, which Bovay called a "swindle." It proposed extending slavery into the new Kansas and Nebraska territories. "We went into the little meeting Whigs, Free Soilers, and Democrats," Bovay later recalled. "We came out Republicans, and were the first Republicans in the Union." The name, he said, was selected for its "charm and prestige." Less than two years later, a convention was held in Pittsburgh to establish a national organization under the Republican banner; Greeley and Abraham Lincoln were among those who attended.

"Fightin' Bob" La Follette's state administration took on the railroads, levying the first railroad property tax and regulating their rates within Wisconsin. He used a tragedy from an earlier generation—the terrible forest fire that killed about twelve hundred timber workers in northern Wisconsin on the same night in 1871 that the Great Fire killed nine hundred fewer people in Chicago—to begin safety and regulatory reform of an industry that had denuded most of the state's virgin forest. In Peshtigo today is a museum that recalls the inferno—the worst fire disaster in American history. In 1924, La Follette, while a U.S. senator, ran for president as an isolationist and trustbuster. He received almost five million popular votes but the electoral votes of only one state: his own. In Madison, Old Bob had spread the gospel of the "Wisconsin Idea"—turning ideals and fresh concepts espoused on university campuses into concrete government programs. He had appointed a "brain trust" of University of Wisconsin professors to advise him on legislation and state administration. "La Follette was more than a great man," John Gunther wrote in his book, *Inside U.S.A.* "He became a myth. His technique was, by and large, to take up specific concrete issues [such as the imposition of an inheritance tax, or the assault on the power of the railroads] one at a time." The Progressive legacy included the establishment of recall elections, broadened home rule for towns and cities, debt relief for farmers, and the beginnings of what became one of the nation's most prestigious primary elections.

Although Progressives lost some elections in the 1920s and again in the '30s, and the party voted itself out of existence in 1946 after most of its conservative members (including Young Bob La Follette) slipped back into the Republican Party while liberal-leaning Progressives went to the Democrats, the aura of progressivist "good government" still permeates the state. Wisconsin voters have little tolerance for political chicanery and quickly turn against any politician who is even slightly tarred by impropriety in office. The state's reputation for fiscal prudence was enhanced during William Proxmire's thirty-two years in the United States Senate, where he skewered wasteful or frivolous government programs by presenting them his uncoveted "Golden Fleece" awards.

Given all this, Wisconsinites are inevitably asked, how did you send to the U.S. Senate a reactionary, "red-baiting" county judge who faked a combat record in the late 1940s and early '50s? They respond that Joseph McCarthy was a gregarious campaigner, full of good humor, when he was first elected in 1946, and that he gave few inklings of a darker nature. Later, McCarthy's witch-hunts for the "205 known Communists in the State Department" were a part of the milieu of the times, when U.S. atomic secrets had been compromised and Communist regimes had subjugated parts of Eastern Europe from which many Wisconsinites or their parents had moved.

Tiny Stockholm was even teenier in the 19-teens. The new store building on the left was later moved and is today an Amish store in the artsy Mississippi River town.

Families took to the high ground—and even rooftops—during the Chippewa River flood of 1884. Because of heavy winter snowfall in northern Wisconsin, flooding is a periodic menace downstream.

Like the rest of the country, Wisconsin was weary of war and sacrifice, and tired of drumbeats for reform. It wanted a piece of the good life and was responsive to the appeal of conservatives like McCarthy. (It was in 1946, as well, that Richard Nixon was first elected in California.) Young Bob La Follette had perhaps overstayed his time in Washington. Wisconsinites thought he was spending too much time on Senate committee work, and not enough checking in back home. "McCarthy is an S.O.B.," went a refrain of the times, "but he's *our* S.O.B." Even so, he defeated La Follette by only a few thousand votes.

By the middle of the twentieth century, Wisconsin, and even Milwaukee, had lost much of their German flavor. Before World War I in Milwaukee and the Fox River Valley, German newspapers were far more influential, and more widely read, than English papers; German was taught in public school; and German was the language of hundreds of churches. Prior to America's entry into the war, German-Americans were as enthusiastic in their support of war relief for Germany as others were in helping war-torn England and France. The U.S. declaration of war against their homeland changed German-Americans' prosperous enclave forever. Suspected and sometimes vilified—despite abundant evidence of their loyalty to their new country—German-Americans saw their influence wane in the community they had largely created. "A tragic tide of hatred and anti-German bigotry swept the country, leaving once-proud German settlements, like Milwaukee, quivering in its wake," wrote Ellen Langill and Dave Jensen in the commemorative history *Milwaukee 150*. "The German language, once the most popular in all the city's schools, became odious to many people who insisted that their children enroll in French classes instead. From a high point of 30,000 students enrolled in German in Milwaukee schools in 1916, the number fell to only 400 two years later." To survive,

German merchants found it necessary to post signs reading, "English spoken here." Most German newspapers were gone by 1930, and Milwaukee's Socialist Party was torn to bits by the furor. A generation later during World War II, although pro-Nazi "Bund" activities—largely organized by recent arrivals from the chaotic Weimar Republic rather than by second- or third-generation German-Americans—grabbed headlines, most young men of German heritage enlisted or were drafted, and served the United States honorably, and their families bought war bonds in the same proportions as their neighbors.

African-Americans in search of factory work streamed to Wisconsin's industrial cities from the South after World War II. But jobs proved to be more elusive than in Detroit, Chicago, or Cleveland. The newcomers faced racism, but also entrenched hiring and union apprenticeship systems that favored the employment of relatives and friends. "Last hired" blacks in the 1950s would become the "first fired" casualties of factory downsizings and closings like the demise of Kenosha's American Motors, beginning in the 1970s. Blacks today make up about a third of Milwaukee's population, principally in former German neighborhoods north of Wisconsin Avenue and west of the Milwaukee River. Most Germans—and their churches, private schools, and all but a few restaurants and sausage shops—headed for the suburbs. Less affluent Polish neighborhoods on Milwaukee's South Side, by contrast, remain Polish, often in tight proximity with a growing Hispanic population. In their *Book of America,* Neal R. Peirce and Jerry Hagstrom quote a South Side priest as observing in 1980, "My funerals are all in Polish. My weddings and baptisms are all Latino."

The most evident vestige of the pervasive influence of Germans in eastern Wisconsin is architectural—in stately, elaborately trimmed structures like Milwaukee's City Hall and the

Wisconsinites delight in their snowy winters. Snowshoeing was in the plans at the Delos Moon home in Eau Claire in the 1910s; it's unclear what purpose the drum at the left was to serve.

Pabst family mansion, and in large wooden duplexes. This was the German route to home ownership: live in half a house, and rent out the other half (plus a worker's cottage out back) to pay the mortgage. On Milwaukee's South Side, "Polish flats" are more common. These are humble wooden apartments built atop brick storefronts. But multiunit apartment buildings in the New York or Chicago mold are relatively rare.

Milwaukee and Madison rank third and fourth, respectively, among Wisconsin's Top Ten travel destinations. First is Wisconsin Dells, a seven-mile stretch of the Wisconsin River flanked by steep, sculpted cliffs. Families come for the water slides, small theme parks, and miniature golf courses as well as for a splash in the river. Second is Door County, the picturesque thumb of land that juts north from Green Bay. Its 250-mile stretch of Lake Michigan bluffs and beaches, multiple lighthouses, and acres of apple and cherry orchards is endearing enough; add the specialty shops, flaming fish boils, and cozy guest houses, and Door County looks for all the world like Nantucket lifted inland.

Some other Top Ten Wisconsin attractions are the rugged Northwoods, including two national forests and a twenty-nine-mile National Scenic Byway; the Great Mississippi River Road, a three-hundred-mile route along locks and limestone bluffs, cheese factories, and even buffalo ranches; Lake Geneva, on whose shores President Calvin Coolidge once kept a Summer White House, and where Chicago society built "cottages"—most of them still visible only from the lake itself—after that city's Great Fire; and Spring Green. Or rather, two venues just outside town— Taliesin, Frank Lloyd Wright's six-hundred-acre estate built into the hills of the Wisconsin River Valley, and the House on the Rock, dreamer Alex Jordan's creation set on a sixty-foot chimney of rock in the 1940s. Today the House on the Rock is just part of a two-hundred-acre complex

Prosperous Rice Lake's sawmill and family-owned creamery were both the world's largest in the 1920s; another factory turned out 3.5 million cans of peas in 1924, when Wisconsin produced half the nation's output.

of bizarre rooms, streets, gardens, and buildings, which can take almost half a day to tour. Sights include the world's largest carousel—all of it inside—and a space full of pipe organs and automated music machines. There is also a room with 3,264 windows that seems to teeter two hundred feet out and over the Wyoming Valley below. Green Bay, whose Lambeau Field stadium and Packer Hall of Fame are the best-known draws, and Apostle Islands National Lakeshore, a scenic chain of Lake Superior isles, are other top tourist magnets.

Motor tours of Wisconsin often begin in the southeast, along Interstate 94 through Kenosha and Racine to Milwaukee; or Interstate 90 from Rockford to Beloit, Janesville, and Madison; or east from Beloit along Interstate 43 into the Lake Country that includes Lake Geneva and Williams Bay. The latter is the site of the powerful forty-inch refracting telescope at the University of Chicago's Yerkes Observatory. In the southeast, too, are Old World Wisconsin in Eagle, and Watson's Wild West Museum and General Store in Elkhorn. Old World Wisconsin, one of six State Historical Society sites across Wisconsin, is a vast outdoor museum of immigrant farm and village life. At the Wild West Museum, owner Doug Watson tells rip-roaring cowboy tales, but the feast is visual: an amazing collection of general store items, elk and bison heads, guns, and horse collars in a big, renovated barn. As a visiting newspaper reporter put it, "You don't know where to look first!"

Milwaukee, a city of ninety-six square miles and roughly six hundred thousand people, calls itself "The Genuine American City" because of its diversity. Those keeping track of the number of identifiable ethnic groups in town stopped counting at 110 a few years ago. An architectural treasure trove, Milwaukee offers far more than festivals, ballgames, brats, and beer (though the city *is* littered with new brewpubs and sports bars, as well as fine Continental, African, and, of

Madeline Island in Lake Superior historically has been the spiritual home of the Ojibwa (Chippewa) people. It was an important French fur-trading post and missionary center. Of late it is a favorite tourist destination.

course, German restaurants). Its symphony orchestra is world-acclaimed; its vibrantly restored Third Ward has become a café, gallery, antiquing, and experimental-theatre scene; its Riverwalk of shops, restaurants, water taxis, and even gondolas keeps expanding; and its new museum complex, opened in 1996, drew raves as a "Milwaukee makeover" from the national newspaper *USA Today*. Ground was broken that same year for a new, $250 million baseball park. Milwaukee has not only a children's museum, but also free summertime jazz concerts in Cathedral Square Park, beautiful horticultural exhibits under Mitchell Park's three glass domes, and even a clown museum and an annual, old-fashioned circus street parade. Milwaukee is big but manageable, cultured but a lot of fun.

Madison, a city one-third Milwaukee's size, became Wisconsin's capital by hook if not crook. While the first territorial legislature was meeting in tiny Belmont in southwest Wisconsin, trying to decide upon a permanent capital, established cities like Fond du Lac, Platteville, and Green Bay jostled for support. All the while, Judge James Dody, who with Michigan's governor had bought undeveloped land on a narrow isthmus between glacial lakes Mendota and Menona eighty miles west of Milwaukee, was determined to see the capital put there. So he laid out the plans for a city and offered lots at bargain prices to precisely the right people: the legislators themselves. On the day that Madison City—as this wild, uninhabited place was called—was chosen, only one legislator had ever seen it.

When Wisconsin became a state in 1848, Madison had a grid of streets named for signers of the U.S. Constitution, a leaky wooden capitol building, and authority from the new state legislature to establish a land-grant university in town. Madison was, and, so far as anyone knows, still is the only city in the world built on an isthmus. Since then, it has grown to become the intellectual nexus of Wisconsin, a place that has variously been chosen America's best place to live (*Money* magazine, 1996), one of the Top Ten "canoe towns" (*Paddler* magazine, 1995), and "No. 3 among Great Places to Raise a Family" (*Parenting*, May 1997). Madison's "Museum Mile," two hundred parks, and thirteen public beaches help explain the city's appeal. A short drive away are Spring Green's Taliesin and House on the Rock; ethnic villages in Blue Mounds, New Glarus, and Mount Horeb; Wisconsin Dells; a fascinating railway museum offering steam train rides to visitors in little North Freedom; and the world's largest array of circus parade wagons and calliopes, plus a miniature circus and other memorabilia at Circus World Museum in Baraboo.

Because of a student population approaching forty thousand, plus the army of state office workers in town, Madison is a vibrant political and social setting. Still haunted by memories of campus demonstrations against Dow Chemical Company–sponsored research and the presence of R.O.T.C. recruiters on campus in the tumultuous 1960s—protests in which the "U's" Math-Science building was bombed and a researcher killed—some Wisconsinites still talk about the capital city as if it were a seething cauldron of radicalism. In truth, it has been as moderately Democratic for thirty or more years as most of the rest of Wisconsin has been moderately Republican. Even Paul Soglin, a former "U" student activist—originally from Chicago—elected mayor on an avowedly "hippie" ticket in 1973, quietly improved the city's transportation system and directed the revitalization of old State Street.

In 1994, the U.S. Travel Data Center reported that just two percent of American vacationers planned to visit a historic site; by 1996, two years later, the figure had risen to fifty-two percent, a testament to the increasing pull of heritage tours and historic places. In Wisconsin there is no place better to satisfy this curiosity than to travel the Great Mississippi River Road. There one finds settlements like Hudson on the Saint Croix, a Mississippi tributary. Founded in 1840 by fur traders, Hudson was a lumber camp and steamboat center, and it still boasts a number of fashionable Victorian-era homes. Prescott, too, an old shipping and lumber center, is partial to Greek Revival architecture. Little Pepin is the birthplace of Laura Ingalls Wilder, whose life and writings are recounted at the Pepin Historical Museum. In the former Swiss village of Alma, stone walls and stairs connect the village's only two parallel roads beneath a five-hundred-foot bluff. In Prairie du Chien stands Villa Louis, considered one of the most authentically furnished Victorian homes in America. Inland, Mineral Point was the center of Cornish culture. There and at Pendarvis, Cornish miners lived and dug for lead ore.

Western Wisconsin, around Warrens, is also cranberry country. There's a big museum, Cranberry Expo, in town, and a Cranberry Festival each September. Cranberry marshes are most visible on a twenty-three-mile wetlands route past the marshes and reservoirs where not just cranberries, but also sphagnum moss, are grown. The moss is sterile and can hold twenty times its weight in water. Water in the marshes is a dark tea color, the result of acid leeched from tamarack trees whose branches hang overhead. Bicycle tours through the area, and on the La Crosse River State Trail along abandoned Chicago and North Western Railroad lines between Sparta and Medary, are also popular diversions. Sparta accentuated its passion for biking by erecting a shiny, thirty-foot-high, fiberglass wheelman aboard the "World's Largest Bike" in a park in 1997.

Woodsmen made their own entertainment in the early lumber camps for there were no movies, radio, or nearby towns of any size to relieve tedium. The fellow at the left danced to the fiddler's tune.

La Crosse, Wisconsin's largest Mississippi River city, got its name when French fur traders, visiting a Winnebago campsite, saw Indians playing a game that reminded them of the French sport *la crosse*. The city is home to the G. Heilemann Brewing Company (now owned by Stroh's), one of the nation's leading regional brewers, where not only Heilemann's own Old Style brand but also beers custom-brewed for clients in several states are produced. Some of the beer is stored in six giant tanks that look like grain elevators, painted with Old Style logos to resemble the "World's Largest Six Pack." Together, they hold enough brew to fill more than seven million twelve-ounce cans. Docked on the Mississippi is the *Julia Belle Swain*, a replica of the original steam-operated stern paddlewheelers of the 1880s. One of only six remaining steam-powered passenger boats still plying the river—and the only one based on the Upper Mississippi—*Julia Belle Swain* escorts the New Orleans-based *Delta Queen* and *Mississippi Queen* into Riverside Park during the larger boats' occasional visits to La Crosse.

Other good-sized cities in western Wisconsin—Eau Claire, Chippewa Falls, and Menomonie—owe their development to Big Timber, though Eau Claire today ships as many or more tons of cigars, tires, paper products, and composite fireplace logs as it does boards. The broad Chippewa River is one of the state's most beautiful and also most readily navigated by kayak and canoe.

The Ojibwa, or Chippewas, moved to Wisconsin's Lake Superior shore from the east. They found the beauty and abundance of wild rice, deer, bear, and fur-bearing muskrat and beaver irresistible.

Northwest Wisconsin is still sparsely settled, though remote counties like Vilas, below Michigan's Upper Peninsula, have seen dramatic growth in year-round residents as part of what some describe as an "antimetropolitan" migration. Fishing and hunting are divine in these Northwoods, a fact not lost on sportsmen from eastern Ohio to western Iowa, who gladly make the trek north to try their chances during Wisconsin's open seasons. In Hayward, there's even the National Fresh Water Fishing Hall of Fame, complete with a giant fiberglass muskie into whose jaws visitors are welcome to walk, and an impressive collection of anglers' artifacts. In wintertime, snowmobiles by the thousands crisscross the region, sometimes more frequently than do automobiles. It was on a private, secluded lake near Couderay that Chicago mobster Al Capone relaxed with his pals and molls, flew in high-quality Canadian booze by seaplane throughout Prohibition, and hid out—not from G-men but from other gangsters bent on muscling into his turf.

Frigid Lake Superior laps, or, just as often, freezes against the northern Wisconsin shoreline. Across the lake's green water from drowsy Bayfield loom the twenty-two Apostle Islands. From some of them came the high-quality brownstone blocks that built much of Manhattan's Upper East and West Sides. The Ice Age National Scenic Trail snakes through Barron and Rusk counties, opening to visitors the marsh-studded remnants of the last gargantuan glacier, fifteen thousand years ago. Iron ore was the "red gold" of the North Country, and in Iron County, near the tiny town of Pence, is a stark reminder of the iron boom and the bust that followed—the abandoned Plummer Mine Headframe, standing back in the woods as a lonely memorial to the miners and their families who built the mighty Penokee Iron Range.

In north central Wisconsin, the Fox and Wolf rivers drain into Lake Winnebago, Wisconsin's largest inland lake. Prosperous cities that surround it, including Oshkosh and Fond du Lac, grew as mill towns for northern timber. Workers cut and finished the wood and sent it on to

Great Lakes towns for shipbuilding and transport to eastern cities. Today Oshkosh maintains one of the world's busiest airports, not because of the city's size but because sport and stunt flyers—as well as builders of their own airplanes of the class the government calls "experimental"—land to visit the Experimental Aircraft Association Air Adventure Museum and to join in the EAA's mass, once-a-year "fly-in." Another Fox River Valley city, Appleton, was built on paper, or rather, the money that paper milled there brought in. Giant companies like Kimberly-Clark and Menasha Corporation rose in a line along the river. Growing up there, too, were two disparate showmen—rabbi's son Harry Houdini and rabble-rousing Joe McCarthy, the son of an immigrant Irish farmer.

Below the Door Peninsula and above Milwaukee are the Lake Michigan port cities of Manitowoc and Sheboygan, as well as a manufacturing dynamo in little Kohler. Great sailing schooners, and later, submarines and landing craft, were built at Manitowoc. The nation's most extensive collection of Great Lakes history, archaeology, and artifacts is housed in the Wisconsin Maritime Museum there, and a submarine tour is part of the visitor experience. From the port at Sheboygan—once an even more Germanic city than Milwaukee—products from Wisconsin and beyond are shipped east across the Great Lakes to Buffalo, and onto the Erie Canal. Just outside Sheboygan, the Kohler family built an empire supplying porcelained cups and plates, then toilets, bathtubs, and sinks. The residence hotel that once housed Kohler's immigrant porcelain workers is now the five-diamond American Club Resort.

Wisconsin is rarely flashy. Tradition matters, and steady marks its course. The state is sophisticated yet naturally wild, ruggedly individualistic but socially involved, and reverent towards antiquity but open to new people and ideas—all at the same time. It's is an upbeat, optimistic place, where the Wisconsin state motto fits the mood. It reads, simply: "Forward."

Green Bay Packers quarterback Bart Starr lunges for the winning touchdown against Dallas in the 1967 NFL championship game. Played in subzero temperatures, it is remembered as the "Ice Bowl."

OVERLEAF: *The Riverwalk helped revitalize downtown Milwaukee. A $10-million expansion in the mid-1990s added more shops, cultural venues, and restaurants. Gondolas and water taxis now traverse the area.*

Looming City Hall embodies the muscular, Old World flavor of Milwaukee. The building, with its Flemish Renaissance clock tower (left), was designed by Henry C. Koch and completed in 1895. Its massive size and hefty construction budget stamped Milwaukee as a city to be reckoned with, and the building remains the city's most recognizable downtown landmark, meeting spot, and jewel of its skyline. Its trapezoidal shape—necessitated by its location on a pie-shaped lot at the angled intersection of two downtown streets—is evident in the elaborate, extensively renovated interior (opposite), which bears a striking resemblance to the historic city jail in Dublin, Ireland. The neighborhood around City Hall has reawakened with shops, restaurants, and even in-town residences returning the "life" to downtown nightlife.

Beer made Milwaukee famous, but it was grain that first made it rich. In the 1870s, Milwaukee shipped more wheat than any other port in the world. Grain futures, or crops bought and sold for future delivery, were traded in a spectacular downtown Grain Exchange Room (above). The grand room—which introduced the world's first trading pit— is three stories high, and features murals, frescoes by Peter Almini of Chicago, a Japanese-style smoking room, and a spectator balcony. It declined for a time, and workers punched holes in Almini's painted ceiling to hang steel wires for a false ceiling. But the building was grandly restored in the early 1980s and is now used for receptions and other occasions. A favorite hallmark of the city's nightscape is the Milwaukee Gas Company Building's rooftop "flame" (opposite) that changes color according to the weather forecast.

Broadway Street (above) in Milwaukee's historic Third Ward, south of downtown between the Milwaukee River and Lake Michigan, is an old warehouse district that has been converted into theaters, lofts, antique shops, and galleries. The city also added period-style street-lighting and improved sidewalks. The building with the elaborate fire escapes is the 1902 American Candy Company Building, designed by Charles Crane. Across the street is the old Engine Company No. 10 firehouse (right), marked with a sculpture created in 1990 by Michael Capser. Fire destroyed virtually all Third Ward warehouses in 1892, but the buildings—many of which are now nationally registered historic places—were quickly replaced.

ENGINE COMPANY
No. 10
Created By:
Michael Capser
Commissioned By:
Thomas M. Wamser
June 10th, 1990

Mader's (opposite) on Old World Third Street in downtown Milwaukee has been voted the most German restaurant in North America. The 1902 establishment is a local institution, known as much for its gemütlichkeit (good fellowship) as for its trademark sauerkraut balls, liver dumpling soup, and Rhine sauerbraten. The story of another German tradition— sausage making— is told at the "Streets of Old Milwaukee" Exhibit (left) at the Milwaukee Public Museum. For more than a century, the museum has featured walk-through galleries that display the world's cultural and natural heritage. The museum owns more than six million specimens and artifacts. In Dinosaur Hall, which holds the world's largest known dinosaur skull, and elsewhere throughout the museum, are "stop spots" where educators are available to assist in interpreting exhibits.

In 1871, the Wisconsin Legislature authorized a water system for Milwaukee. The city built a pumping station with intake from Lake Michigan, a tower—now called the Old North Point Water Tower (right)—a reservoir, and fifty-five miles of water mains. The 175-foot water tower—designed by Charles Gombert— kept its giant stand-pipe from freezing. It remained in service from 1874 to 1963. The Saint Josephat Basilica (opposite) in South Milwaukee, magnificently restored in the 1990s, is owned, not by the Archdiocese of Milwaukee, but by the Conventual Fran-scican Friars, Sisters, and parishioners. The Franciscans spent $5.5 million to beautify the interior of the structure, which was built in 1888 using materials from an abandoned U.S. Post Office. It has long served a largely Polish-American congregation.

In the 1890s, Captain Frederick Pabst was a brewer, philanthropist, and art patron. Following the decline of Milwaukee's wheat trade, Pabst, along with brewers named Schlitz, Miller, and Blatz, increased their fortunes by shipping their products far from home. Pabst built an opulent Victorian home (above), now a museum that is one of Milwaukee's most-visited attractions. The Pabst Mansion incorporated fine wood carvings, plaster detailing, and ornamental ironwork. It also utilized the city's famous cream-colored brick, and for a time Milwaukee was known as the "Cream City" because of the many structures that did likewise. Later generations of wealthy Milwaukeeans built showplace homes like the one pictured (right) along North Lake Drive along Lake Michigan. Many of these manor homes have since been subdivided.

After the Great Fire of 1871 leveled much of Chicago, a number of wealthy Chicagoans—notably the Wrigleys of chewing gum fame—decided to construct sumptuous mansions away from the city on Lake Geneva in southern Wisconsin. Today not just Lake Geneva's Main Street is lined with these homes (above); so is the lake itself. Many great estates, which cannot be seen from the road, were supplied by lake steamers like the Louise (left). Some have been turned into tour boats for champagne, jazz, and even ice-cream cruises past the fabulous lakefront homes. The town of Lake Geneva remains a favorite weekend and holiday haunt for visiting Chicagoans.

On Bob Pearce's farm in Fontana (opposite), the corn is not quite as high as an elephant's eye but it thrives most years in Wisconsin's agreeable summer climate. Unlike Iowa sweet corn to the southwest, most Wisconsin corn is destined not for picnic tables, but for silos to feed the state's huge dairy herds. Farms are so numerous in Wisconsin that they can seem mundane—until you catch a special moment such as the sunrise over cornfields near Beloit (top left). Sunflowers, like this patch near Darien (bottom left), are also a growing crop, especially in relatively warm southeast Wisconsin. As in all Midwest states, the number of farms in Wisconsin has been declining—and their size increasing—since the 1920s. Today the average Wisconsin farm exceeds two hundred acres.

45

The First Congregational United Church of Christ in Elkhorn (above) marked 150 years of service in 1993. The original steeple, above the existing open bell tower, was a tall spire that had to be removed in 1936 due to rotting timbers. The 1897 Yerkes Observatory (right) in Williams Bay is a research institution operated by the University of Chicago's Department of Astronomy and Astrophysics. Investigators not only explore the solar system and distant galaxies here, they also design and test sensitive instruments for telescopes throughout the world. The observatory is named for Chicago transit tycoon Charles Tyson Yerkes. Edwin Blashfield of New York painted "Resources of Wisconsin" at the top of the Wisconsin Capitol dome (overleaf)—one of the largest domes, by volume, in the world.

The Wisconsin Supreme Court moved into the State Capitol (opposite) when it opened in 1911. Despite the serious tenor of deliberations inside the beautiful hearing room, the architect added a whimsical touch above the entryway: a badger-head sculpture peering out on the hallway below. The University of Wisconsin–Madison (above) is the fourth-largest and one of the top-ranked universities in the nation. Students hit the books—or catch a nap—outside Bascom Hall, the university's administration building. Bronze models of Wisconsin's citizen-soldiers, made from head and body casts of real people in New York and Madison, comprise a "Tribute to Freedom" (overleaf) in the window of the Wisconsin Veterans Museum, across from the Wisconsin Capitol. Shown, left to right, are a Civil War cavalryman on horseback, a Civil War infantryman, a Spanish-American War infantryman, and a Red Cross nurse.

Graceful Victorian homes, such as this one (left), dot the Monroe Street Shopping Area, close to the University of Wisconsin–Madison campus. The neighborhood attracts many faculty members and their families, a number of whom are assiduous gardeners. Watertown's eight-sided, five-story Octagon House (above) was built in the early 1850s by pioneer John Richards, an attorney, miller, and early Watertown mayor. With its fifty-seven rooms, it was probably the largest single-family residence in pre-Civil War Wisconsin, if not in the entire Midwest. Inside is a dizzying, cantilevered, spiral staircase. On the grounds is the building that housed the first kindergarten in the United States—begun by Margarethe Meyer Schurz, wife of famous German-American statesman Carl Schurz.

Historic interpreters work dried clover for livestock (above) and harvest horseradishes (right) at Old World Wisconsin, the State Historical Society's outdoor museum in Eagle. The park, which covers 576 acres—four times the size of Colonial Williamsburg in Virginia—examines immigrant farm and village life in a number of ethnic settings (Polish, Finnish, and German among them) and across ten farms and a crossroads village. Weekend events include temperance rallies, town hall meetings, Civil War encampments, and hands-on activities for children. "History is a tale with many versions," Old World Wisconsin's visitors' guide points out. "Historians disagree about the past, just as people experienced the past in different ways. Old World Wisconsin is a version of the past, not the past itself."

Colorful wagons were once the harbinger of fun as they carried the circus down Main Street in every decent-sized burg in America before and after the turn of the twentieth century. Today dozens of these elaborately carved wagons, including this elephant wagon (left), can be found at Circus World Museum in Baraboo. It took Paul LaReau fifteen hundred hours to craft the styrofoam-and-wire model of the U.S. Capitol (above) now on display— along with models of the Statue of Liberty, the Taj Mahal, the Alamo, and other structures—at LaReau's World of Miniature Buildings near Pardeeville. In North Freedom, this 1907 steam locomotive and dozens of other locomotives and vintage rail cars are preserved at the remarkable Mid-Continent Railway Museum (overleaf).

One silo was not enough for this farm (above) near the town of Plain. It has three to store silage for its dairy herd. About 40 percent of the nation's cheese and 20 percent of its butter come from Wisconsin, and the state is a top producer of condensed, evaporated, dried, and malted milk, as well as ice cream. Since Sparta, in western Wisconsin, lays claim to the title of "Bicycling Capital of America," it makes sense that the town would display the "World's Largest Bike" (opposite), a thirty-foot fiberglass model with appropriate rider, erected in 1997. The nation's first rails-to-trails path—in which an old railroad right-of-way is converted to a biking and hiking trail—originated in Sparta. The thirty-two mile Elroy-Sparta Trail stretches along an abandoned Chicago & North Western Railroad bed and passes through three rock tunnels.

On land near Spring Green, first settled by his Welsh ancestors, fabled architect Frank Lloyd Wright built Taliesin (opposite), one of the world's most famous homes, begin-ning in 1911. He con-sidered it to be the supreme "natural house," blended so deftly into native sur-roundings that he said "it was not so easy to tell where pavements and walls left off and ground began." Steel beams recovered from a World War II aircraft carrier provided the support for the soaring "Birdwalk" balcony, added in 1953, that juts far out from the house and provides a match-less view of the valley. At Taliesin, Wright surrounded himself with architects-in-training, and work was always in progress. Wright took inspira-tion from the estate's grounds and peaceful lake (above). This is ancient topography, as the Ice Age glaciers missed this part of Wisconsin.

Wisconsin's No. 1 individual tourist attraction is the House on the Rock, near Spring Green. The overall experience of this phenomenon, the eccentric life work of Alex Jordan of Madison, almost defies description. There's an incredible indoor carousel (left)—the world's largest, indoor or out—which features all manner of animals except horses! There is also an organ room, a Mikado music machine, a "Streets of Yesterday" exhibit, hundreds of bisque dolls, and more. Outside, sculptures (above) are appropriately bizarre. In the little settlement of Belmont (overleaf), Wisconsin's first territorial capitol building, on the right, has been preserved. The building on the left was the residence of the territory's first chief justice.

71

Mineral Point (top right) was "the place where Wisconsin began" in the 1820s, when prospectors swarmed over the hills of present-day southwest Wisconsin looking for lead. A mining camp around the diggings eventually became Mineral Point, which today has streets with colorful names like "Shake Rag." Pictured is the Green Lantern Antique Shop on High Street. Early Swiss settlers built New Glarus, and their pioneer lives are remembered at the Swiss Village Museum. Shown is an 1854 Swiss settler's cabin (bottom right). Swiss architecture now abounds throughout "America's Little Switzerland." Mount Horeb (opposite) is home to several of Mike Feeney's carved trolls, which, legend has it, are keepers of the minerals of the earth and associated with good luck. Trolls, including this specimen outside Open House Imports, have four fingers and four toes.

In southwest Wisconsin is a collection of more than two thousand varieties of mustard, of all things, at the Mount Horeb Mustard Museum (above). Why? Only a visit makes sense of the story, but it has to do with a former Wisconsin assistant attorney general and certain Mount Horebians' interest in medicinal mustard plasters. One of Wisconsin's leading factories is the Alp and Dell (right) in Monroe. Pictured are curing baby Swiss rounds. In Blue Mounds is Little Norway, whose main house (overleaf) was built in Norway in 1892–93 for display at the World's Columbian Exposition in Chicago. It was moved to Lake Geneva, disassembled in 1935, shipped to Blue Mounds, and reassembled.

Blue Mounds takes its name from two bluish hills that are landmarks in south central Wisconsin. Both were settled by lead miner Ebenezer Brigham. Cave of the Mounds (above), beneath them, was accidentally discovered in 1939 by workers blasting limestone from a quarry. The explosion revealed a limestone cavern more than twenty feet high, opening into other subterranean rooms containing numerous mineral formations. The cave began to form about a million and a half years ago when the magnesium-rich limestone, called "Galena dolomite," was still beneath the water table. The stone grotto and shrines (opposite) in little Dickeyville in southwest Wisconsin were built by Father Matthias Wernerus, pastor of the local Catholic parish. He dedicated his handiwork to two American ideals: love of God and love of country. The grotto's colored glass, gems, seashells, and other ornaments were collected all over the world.

The Julia Belle Swain (right) is one of only six steamboats still operating on the upper Mississippi. The boat, constructed in 1971, cruises for one or two days out of Riverside Park in La Crosse. The boat has been featured in three movies, including The Wild West. La Crosse's G. Heilemann Brewing Company, now owned by Stroh's, began aging its Old Style-brand beer in "The World's Largest Six-Pack" tanks (above) in 1969. It would take a customer 120 years, drinking one twelve-ounce can of beer every hour, twenty-four hours a day, every day of the year, to equal the beer in one of these giant "cans."

NO
TRESPASSING
VIOLATORS WILL
BE PROSECUTED

The Hixon House (opposite) in La Crosse was built in 1860 when millwork indicated the quality of a house. It was constructed by Gideon Hixon, a native Vermonter who prospered tinning roofs and struck out to find his fortune in the West. He found it in La Crosse running a sawmill. The Hixon House's gardens have been restored to the carefully pruned look of the 1880s. Upriver is the tiny town of Stockholm, which has become a popular art and antiques center. Amish quilts and furniture are sold at the old store (above) whose building can be seen in an early view on page 13. Stockholm and other small towns along Wisconsin's Great Mississippi River Road lie on or beneath majestic bluffs—once Indian lookout posts—that offer spectacular views of the river and nearby marshes. A hillside park (overleaf) is near Hager City.

High above the town of Hudson amid sandstone bluffs along the Saint Croix River—a wide Mississippi River tributary—are some of the fifteen thousand or so mounds (opposite) built by Woodland People about five thousand years ago. Clay pots and copper objects have been found in some of them, but the exact purpose of the mounds themselves remains uncertain. The bluffs above Hudson are a great vantage point from which to watch the annual Independence Day fireworks upriver in Stillwater, Minnesota. Hundreds of Wisconsin and Minnesota yachtsmen enjoy the sight from their boats anchored in the Saint Croix as well. Downstream on the Mississippi near Pepin is a replica of "The Little House in the Big Woods" (above)—the childhood home of Laura Ingalls Wilder. Wilder wrote a series of internationally acclaimed "Little House" children's books about her family's adventures in several Midwest states.

Farm life is as hard in Wisconsin as it is anywhere else, but visitors to the state can enjoy the bucolic settings created by the hard work. This scene (left) is near Pepin, as is the round barn (above). There were once hundreds of round wood or stone structures in the state when they were a Victorian fashion statement. They were also practical: round barns can deflect high winds, which can make toothpicks of traditional rectangular varieties. Constructing a wooden round barn is tricky; wooden boards must be soaked—usually in a nearby river, sometimes for weeks— before they can be bent around the barn's roof supports or downstairs shell. The sunset scene (overleaf) was captured along Highway 40 near the little community of Bruce in northwest Wisconsin.

The exquisitely restored Mabel Tainter Theater (opposite) in Menomonie features intricate hand stenciling; hand-carved woodwork (and no plasterwork); gleaming brass fixtures; leaded glass windows; and a rare working Steene and Turner tracker pipe organ. Seats come in small, medium, and large! Menomonie enjoys an outstanding performing-arts season as well as an art gallery and an authentic turn-of-the-century public reading room. The theater was constructed in 1889 by lumber baron Andrew Tainter and his wife, Bertha, as a memorial to their daughter, who died at age 19. The Cook-Rutledge Mansion (above) in Chippewa Falls, built in the 1870s with lavish ornamental ironwork and gingerbread trim, was turned into one of Wisconsin's most elegant homes by lumberman Edward Rutledge. Attorney Dayton Cook purchased the home in 1915, and a descendant sold it to the Chippewa County Historical Society in 1973.

The Chippewa Valley Museum and the Paul Bunyan Logging Camp are neighbors in Eau Claire's Carson Park. An authentic early log house (above) is one of many exhibits at the museum. Others include a turn-of-the-century ice cream parlor, a twenty-one-foot dollhouse, an old schoolhouse, an early kitchen from the late 1800s, a room that traces the movements of the Ojibwa (Chippewa) Indian people, and dioramas that describe the rich flora and fauna of the area. Statues of mythical woodsman Paul Bunyan and his blue ox, Babe (opposite), stand before the entrance of the logging camp. A project begun in 1934 by two Eau Claire Kiwanis Club members, the camp preserves many of the early photographs and artifacts of the Chippewa Valley's once-vibrant lumber camps. Among the latter: a cook shanty, bunkhouse, and blacksmith shop. The camp is sustained by donors and Kiwanis volunteers.

One of the nation's most amazing repositories of folk art is Wisconsin Concrete Park (top right) in tiny Phillips. It displays more than two hundred real and mythical characters created out of cement, glass, wood, metal, and stone by Fred Smith, a logger, tavern owner, musician—and self-taught artist. "The Hideout" (bottom right) in Couderay was once Al Capone's Northwoods retreat. Located on a private lake, it was safe from rival gangsters and used to land Canadian "hootch" by seaplane. Capone played poker with "the boys" in this cozy living room. Sinfully rich pies are legendary at Norske's Nook Cafe (opposite) in Osseo. It was named in 1973 for the Norwegian farmers who were "regulars." Piney woods and marshes near Clam Lake (overleaf) are home to elk, bear, and other wildlife.

Scheer's Lumberjack Shows on the Namekagon River in Hayward are a favorite summertime tourist attraction. Contestants compete to stay upright on floating logs (opposite) in a traditional lumberjack sport. Events include speed climbing up spar poles, cross-cut sawing, canoe jousting, ax throwing, and chopping, along with "birling"—the traditional term for the logrolling competition. The camp cook provides music and storytelling as well as a barbecue dinner. "Lumberjack Village" also hosts the annual Lumberjack World Championships. Giant bucksaws, up to six feet in length, slice through twelve-inch aspen logs with the speed of a modern-day power saw. Lumberjacks once climbed trees, cut a notch into which they inserted a long board, then stood on the board as they chopped off the treetop. Sunsets are often magnificent in the Northwoods; this one (above) was captured along the Couderay River.

Washburn, on the peninsula that juts into Lake Superior, is a haven for unusual collectibles shops, including the Wooden Sailor (above). Several have catchy names, including The Old Hippie and The Strip Joint. Near Gilman is a remarkable example of "barn art." Grade-school art teacher Cliff Keepers not only created a Mona Lisa on his brother-in-law's barn, he also garbed the figure in a University of Wisconsin Badger outfit to honor the team's Rose Bowl appearance. Later he painted over that jersey with a Green Bay Packers T-shirt (right) to salute their Super Bowl appearance. Lake Superior (overleaf) is always frigid but entrancing.

Lac (lake) du Flambeau (opposite) in northwest Wisconsin is the centerpiece of one of several Ojibwa (Chippewa) Indian reservations in Wisconsin. Leslie LaBarge (left) is a "jingle-dress dancer" at traditional Chippewa pow-wows, where she dances under her Ojibwa name—"Miskwa Waagoshikwe," or Red Fox Woman. The pow-wows, which are open to visitors, have been a Northwoods tradition since 1951. On the reservation, the George W. Brown Jr. Museum and Cultural Center celebrates Ojibwa culture with dioramas and other exhibits. In Eagle River, "chain saw carver" Ken Schels creates masterpieces out of cedar and white pine at Carl's Wood Art Museum (above).

109

In the tiny crossroads community of Jennings, east of Pelican Lake, is a unique "stovewood"-style building (above). The mercantile building was constructed at the turn of the century by Prussian immigrant John Mecikalski. Stovewood architecture is characterized by short-cut logs that are stacked and joined by mortar or clay. This example of architectural folk art is preserved as a project of the Kohler Foundation. Near Mercer is the Plummer Mine Headframe (opposite), the last such remnant in the Penokee Iron Range. The eighty-foot-tall structure near Pence in Iron County was built in 1904. A headframe is a giant pulley that tugged miners and equipment through several levels, two thousand or more feet into the earth. In twenty-eight years of operation, the Plummer mine yielded 174,000 tons of ore. Dusk (overleaf) illuminates a tranquil scene off U.S. Highway 8 near Woodruff.

You see Green Bay Packer green-and-gold insignias in the most unlikely places all over Wisconsin, as on one of these pumpkins (above) at a fall produce stand. Packer fans are masters of the tailgate party (opposite) outside Lambeau Field, where—in rain, snow, or subfreezing temperatures—"cheeseheads" rustle up bratwursts, beers, and fellowship before every game. The Packers are the only community-owned franchise in the National Football League. Another beloved symbol of the state is the badger. This feisty caricature (right) looms above a defunct petting zoo near the town of Aniwa, east of Wausau. Behind the Red Mill Colonial Shop in Little Hope, near Waupaca, is a covered bridge (overleaf), built in 1970 by Early American craftsman Kenneth Schroeder, who fashioned it after a nineteenth-century New Hampshire model.

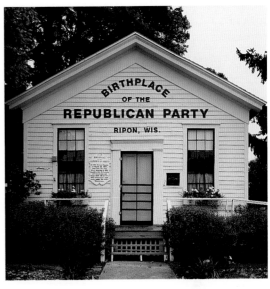

Judy Larson (left) offers a daily show and ninety-minute tour at Larson's Famous Clydesdales farm near Ripon. Shown is Big Jon, one of the gentle giants who weighs almost twenty-four hundred pounds. Also in Ripon is the birthplace of the Republican Party (above)—a schoolhouse where a mass meeting of citizens cut away from the established Whigs and Democrats to form a new party in 1854.

Oshkosh, on Lake Winnebago, is home to the Air Adventure Museum (overleaf), a showplace for more than two hundred modern and historical experimental aircraft. "Experimental" is a government designation for planes built by individuals. Each summer, Oshkosh is inundated with planes and pilots from the world over arriving for the annual Experimental Aircraft Association "Fly-in" convention.

In the old flour-
and paper-mill city
of Appleton stands
Hearthstone (oppo-
site), the world's first
home to be lighted
by a central hydroelec-
tric station. The 1882
Victorian mansion
was designed by busi-
nessman Henry J.
Rogers as an architec-
tural showplace. Its
original Thomas A.
Edison light fixtures
and period electroliers
are still used today.

To the north is
Door County, one of
Wisconsin's favorite
destinations for rest,
relaxation, good food,
quaint shops, and
pastoral beauty. The
farm (left) near Insti-
tute is traditional, but
a real Door County
specialty is cherry
groves (above). Tart
Door County cherry
pies are enjoyed
statewide. Apples
grow in abundance
in the county, too.

EAGLE BLUFF
LIGHTHOUSE MUSEUM

OPEN

The 1868 Eagle Bluff lighthouse (opposite) in Peninsula State Park, near Ephraim, was restored and furnished with antiques by the Door County Historical Society with help from the U.S. Coast Guard and Wisconsin Department of National Resources. The lighthouse is one of several still standing in the county. A Door County tradition is the fish boil (above), notably accomplished at the Viking Grill in Ellison Bay. Boiling whitefish became a specialty here in 1961 when trout was in short supply. The fish is boiled with onions and small red potatoes. From the heights above town, one gets a magnificent view (overleaf) of Green Bay—the inlet, not the town—which opens into nearby Lake Michigan. Along the Door Peninsula are charming towns like Egg Harbor and Fish Creek, which are dotted with boutiques, art galleries, and bed-and-breakfast inns reminiscent of Cape Cod.

Index

Page numbers in italics refer to illustrations.

Air Adventure Museum, Oshkosh, 21, *119*
"America's Little Switzerland," 9, *74*
Apostle Islands National Lakeshore, 17, 20
Appleton, 21, *123*

The badger, shown here in stuffed form at the Chippewa Valley Museum in Eau Claire, is a scrappy, sometimes ill-tempered burrowing mammal. Though "badgering" is rarely admired, the creature's resourcefulness—and, early on, its pelt—caught the fancy of Wisconsin pioneers, who made it the state, and the state university's, symbol.

Badgers, *51, 114, 128*
Beer and breweries, 9, 10, 17, 20, 26, 34, *82*
Belmont territorial capital, 18, *71*
Beloit, 9, 17, *45*
Black Hawk War, 11
Blue Mounds, 9, 19, *76, 80*
Bovay, Alvan E., 12

Capitol building, Madison, *11, 46, 51*
Capone, Al, (*see* Hideout)
Carl's Wood Art Museum, Eagle River, *109*
Cave of the Mounds, *80*
Cheese, 9, *76*
Chicago, 10, 12, 16, *43*
Chippewa Falls and Chippewa Valley, 12, 14, 20, 95, *96*
Chippewa Valley Museum, *96, 128*
Circus World Museum, Baraboo, 19, *63*
Cook-Rutledge Mansion, Chippewa Falls, *95*

Davis, Jefferson, 11
Dells Mill, *4*
Dickeyville Grotto, *80*
Dodge, Henry, 11
Dody, Judge James, 18
Door County, 16, 21, *123, 125*

Eagle, 17, *56*
Eagle Bluff lighthouse, *125*
Eagle River, 9, *109*
Eau Claire, *15*, 20, *96, 128*
Elkhorn, 17, *38, 46*
End of the Trail statue, *59*

Feeney, Mike, *74*
First Congregational United Church of Christ, Elkhorn, *46*
Fond du Lac, 18, 20
Fraser, James Earle, *59*
French exploration and heritage, 10–11, 20

German settlement and influence, 12, 14–16, 17–18, *31*
Grain Exchange Room, *26*
Great Mississippi River Road, 16, 19, *85*
Greeley, Horace, 12
Green Bay Packers, 8, 17, 21, *104, 114*

Hayward, *4*, 9, 20, *103*
Hearthstone Mansion, Appleton, *123*
Heilemann, G. Brewing Company, 20, *82*
Hideout, The, 20, *98*
Hixon House, La Crosse, *85*
Holy Hill National Shrine of Mary, *59*
Horicon Marsh, *7*
Houdini, Harry, 7, 21
House on the Rock, The, 16, 19, *71*
Hudson, 19, *89*

Indian treaties, reservations, and employment, 8, 11, *109*

Julia Belle Swain steamboat, 20, *82*

Kenosha, 10, 15, 17
Kohler company and foundation, 10, 21, *110*
Kringles, 9, *38*

La Crosse, 9, 10, 20, *82, 85*
La Follette, Phil, 7, 12
La Follette, Robert A., Jr., 7, 13, 14
La Follette, Robert A., Sr., 7, 12–13

Lac du Flambeau, *109*
Lake Geneva, 16, 17, *43*
Lake Michigan, *8*, 11, 16, 21, 28, 32, *125*
Lake Superior, 11, 17, *17*, 20, *104*
Lake Winnebago, 20–21, *119*
LaReau's World of Miniature Buildings, *63*
Larson's Famous Clydesdales, *119*
Lincoln, Abraham, 11, 12
Little Norway, Blue Mounds, 9, *76*
Logging camps, 18, *19*

Mabel Tainter Theater, Menomonie, *95*
Madeline Island, 17
Mader's Restaurant, Milwaukee, *31*
Madison, *11*, 16, 17, 18–19,*46, 51, 55*
Manitowoc, 21
McCarthy, Joseph, 13–14, 21
Menomonie, 7, 20, *95*
Mid-Continent Railway Museum, North Freedom, 19, *63*
Millie's Restaurants, Delavan, *38*
Milwaukee, 8, 9, 10, 12, 14–16, *17*–18, *21, 25, 26, 28, 31, 32, 34, 37*
Milwaukee County Zoo, *37*
Milwaukee Public Museum, *31*
Mineral Point, 19, *74*
Mississippi River, *4*, 16, 19, *82, 85*
Mitchell Park Horticultural Conservatory, 18, *37*
Mona Lisa barn art, *104*
Mount Horeb, 19, *74, 76*
Mount Horeb Mustard Museum, *76*
Muir, John, *7*

National Fresh Water Fishing Hall of Fame, *4*, 20
New Glarus, 9, *74*
Nicolet, Jean, 10
Norske's Nook Café, Osseo, *98*
Northwoods, 7, 16, 18, 20, *98, 103*

Octagon House, Watertown, *55*
Ojibwa (Chippewa) tribe, *20, 96,109*
Old North Point Water Tower, *32*
Oshkosh, 20–21, *119*

Pabst, Frederick and Pabst Mansion, 15–16, *34*
Paul Bunyan Logging Camp, Eau Claire, *96*
Pearce, Bob (farm), *45*
Pepin, 19, *89, 91*
Plummer Mine Headframe, 20, *110*
Polish settlement, 15, *32*
Portage and Portage Canal, *60*
Prairie du Chien, 10, 19
Progressive Movement, 7, 12–13
Proxmire, William, 13

Racine, 10, 17, *38*
Republican Party founding, 12, *119*
Rice Lake, *16*
Ripon, 12, *119*

Saint Croix River, 19, *89*
Saint Josephat Basilica, *32*
Scheer's Lumberjack Village, *103*
Sheboygan, 21
Sholes, Christopher Latham, *7*
Sparta, 19, *66*
Spring Green, 16, 19, *69, 71*
Stockholm, 13, *85*
"Stovewood" building, Jennings, *110*
Swiss Village Museum, *74*

Thompson, Tommy, *7*
Trolls, New Glarus, *74*

University of Wisconsin at Madison, 10, 12, 18, 19, *51, 55*

Villa Louis, 19

Washburn, *104*
Watson's Wild West Museum, 17, *38*
Waupun, *59*
Wilder, Laura Ingalls, *8*, 19, *89*
Williams Bay, 17
Wisconsin Concrete Park, Phillips, *98*
Wisconsin Dells, 7, 16, *60*
"Wisconsin Idea, The," 12–13
Wisconsin Maritime Museum, 21
Wisconsin name, 11–12
Wisconsin Veterans Museum, Madison, *51*
Wright, Frank Lloyd and Taliesin, 16, 19, *69*

Yerkes Observatory, 17, *46*